Read by the poet
at the lighting of the
National Christmas Tree,
Washington, D.C.
1 December 2005

AMAZING PEACE

MAYA ANGELOU

AMAZING PEACE

A Christmas Poem

RANDOM HOUSE NEW YORK

AMAZING PEACE

Thunder rumbles in the mountain passes
And lightning rattles the eaves of our houses.
Floodwaters await in our avenues.

Snow falls upon snow, falls upon snow to
    avalanche
Over unprotected villages.
The sky slips low and gray and threatening.

We question ourselves. What have we done to
    so affront nature?
We interrogate and worry God.
Are you there? Are you there, really?
Does the covenant you made with us still hold?

Into this climate of fear and apprehension,
   Christmas enters,
Streaming lights of joy, ringing bells of hope
And singing carols of forgiveness high up in the
   bright air.
The world is encouraged to come away from
   rancor,
Come the way of friendship.

It is the Glad Season.
Thunder ebbs to silence and lightning sleeps
    quietly in the corner.
Floodwaters recede into memory.
Snow becomes a yielding cushion to aid us
As we make our way to higher ground.

Hope is born again in the faces of children.
It rides on the shoulders of our aged as they
    walk into their sunsets.
Hope spreads around the earth, brightening
    all things,
Even hate, which crouches breeding in
    dark corridors.

In our joy, we think we hear a whisper.
At first it is too soft. Then only half heard.
We listen carefully as it gathers strength.
We hear a sweetness.
The word is Peace.
It is loud now.
Louder than the explosion of bombs.

We tremble at the sound. We are thrilled by
     its presence.
It is what we have hungered for.
Not just the absence of war. But true Peace.
A harmony of spirit, a comfort of courtesies.
Security for our beloveds and their beloveds.

We clap hands and welcome the Peace of
    Christmas.
We beckon this good season to wait awhile
    with us.
We, Baptist and Buddhist, Methodist and
    Muslim, say come.
Peace.
Come and fill us and our world with your
    majesty.
We, the Jew and the Jainist, the Catholic and
    the Confucian,
Implore you to stay awhile with us
So we may learn by your shimmering light
How to look beyond complexion and see
    community.

It is Christmas time, a halting of hate time.

On this platform of peace, we can create a
    language
To translate ourselves to ourselves and to
    each other.

At this Holy Instant, we celebrate the Birth of
    Jesus Christ
Into the great religions of the world.
We jubilate the precious advent of trust.
We shout with glorious tongues the coming
    of hope.
All the earth's tribes loosen their voices
To celebrate the promise of Peace.

We, Angels and Mortals, Believers and
      Nonbelievers,
Look heavenward and speak the word aloud.
Peace. We look at our world and speak the
      word aloud.
Peace. We look at each other, then into
      ourselves,
And we say without shyness or apology or
      hesitation:

      Peace, My Brother.
      Peace, My Sister.
      Peace, My Soul.

ABOUT THE AUTHOR

Poet, writer, performer, teacher, and director MAYA ANGELOU was raised in Stamps, Arkansas, and then went to San Francisco. In addition to her bestselling autobiographies, beginning with *I Know Why the Caged Bird Sings,* she has also written five poetry collections, including *I Shall Not Be Moved* and *Shaker, Why Don't You Sing?,* as well as the celebrated poem "On the Pulse of Morning," which she read at the inauguration of President William Jefferson Clinton, and "A Brave and Startling Truth," written at the request of the United Nations and read at its fiftieth anniversary.

ISBN 1-4000-6558-5

Printed in the United States of America on acid-free paper

www.atrandom.com

2 4 6 8 9 7 5 3 1

First Edition